DEAR CARTOON LOVERS,

[and any other kind of lovers too, as far as that goes.]

There's a marvelous new school of cartooning: the Brant Parker, Johnny Hart, Bill Rechin School. The creations of these men are, without a doubt, the funniest stuff in the funnies!*

Now Parker and Rechin have spawned the great new comic strip, CROCK, and have stuffed the wonderfully off-beat characters between the covers of this here book you're holding. Great, great stuff!!

Take it from me, you too will fall down laughing

Vir

*ACTUALLY HART, RECHIN AND PARKER ARE FICTITIOUS CHARACTERS I CREATED.

Don Wilder

CROCK

DRAWN BY BILL RECHIN
WRITTEN BY DON WILDER
REWRITTEN AND REDRAWN
BY BRANT PARKER

A FAWCETT GOLD MEDAL BOOK
Fawcett Books, Greenwich, Connecticut

CROCK

© 1977 CBS Publications, The Consumer Publishing
Division of CBS, Inc. All rights reserved

A Fawcett Gold Medal Book published by arrangement with
Field Newspaper Syndicate.

ISBN 0-449-13868-2

Printed in the United States of America

10 9 8 7 6 5 4 3

tuesday

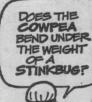

thursday

saturday

thursday

tuesday

thursday

HOW I ENVY YOU, LITTLE BIRD.... YOU CAN FLY TO AND FROM THOSE EXOTIC PLACES.....MARSEILLES. ....SINGAPORE...BAGDAD...

BURRUP!

.... BERNIE'S PIZZA HUT...

tuesday

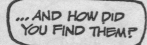

tuesday

thursday

saturday

tuesday

saturday

thursday

thursday

tuesday

thursday

Bill Rechin

saturday

tuesday

tuesday

In the *Wizard of Id* Series

THE KING IS A FINK	1-3709-0	$1.25
THE PEASANTS ARE REVOLTING	1-3671-X	$1.25
REMEMBER THE GOLDEN RULE	1-3717-1	$1.25
THERE'S A FLY IN MY SWILL	1-3687-6	$1.25
THE WONDROUS WIZARD OF ID	1-3648-5	$1.25
THE WIZARD'S BACK	1-3654-X	$1.25
THE WIZARD OF ID—YIELD	1-3653-1	$1.25
THE WIZARD OF ID #8	1-3681-7	$1.25
LONG LIVE THE KING	1-3655-8	$1.25
WE'VE GOT TO STOP MEETING LIKE THIS	1-3633-7	$1.25
EVERY MAN IS INNOCENT UNTIL PROVEN BROKE	1-3650-7	$1.25
I'M OFF TO SEE THE WIZARD	1-3700-7	$1.25